Read-About® Geography

Living in the Savannah

By Linda Bullock

Consultant
Nanci R. Vargus, Ed.D.
Assistant Professor of Literacy
University of Indianapolis, Indianapolis, Indiana

Children's Press®
A Division of Scholastic Inc.
New York   Toronto   London   Auckland   Sydney
Mexico City   New Delhi   Hong Kong
Danbury, Connecticut

Designer: Herman Adler Design
Photo Researcher: Caroline Anderson
The photo on the cover shows Tsavo, Kenya.

Library of Congress Cataloging-in-Publication Data

Bullock, Linda.
  Living in the Savannah / by Linda Bullock.
    p. cm. – (Rookie read-about geography)
  Summary: Introduces the savannah environment and some of the people and
  animals that dwell in savannahs.
    ISBN 0-516-22739-4 (lib. bdg.)   0-516-27327-2 (pbk.)
    1. Savannas–Juvenile literature. [1. Savannas.] I. Title. II.
  Series.
  QH87.7.B86 2003
  577.4'8–dc21
                                    2003003901

CHILDREN'S PRESS, and ROOKIE READ-ABOUT®,
and associated logos are trademarks and or registered trademarks
of Scholastic Library Publishing. SCHOLASTIC and associated logos
are trademarks and or registered trademarks of Scholastic Inc.

1 2 3 4 5 6 7 8 9 10 R 12 11 10 09 08 07 06 05 04 03

The lion roars.

Where does this lion live?

He lives on the African savannah (suh-VAN-uh). A savannah is a grassland.

Baobab tree

The African savannah is wide. Only a few trees grow here.

The baobab (BAY-oh-bab) tree grows here. It lives a long, long time.

Many animals live on
the savannah.

Zebras, rhinos, and hippos
eat grasses. Giraffes eat
leaves from the acacia
(uh-KAY-shuh) trees.

Zebras

The savannah is hot and sometimes dry. Fires can burn the grass.

Elephants dig for water in dry riverbeds. Other animals come to drink at the water hole.

People also live on the
savannah. Some Masai
(mah-SIGH) and other
African people live on farms.

Other people move herds
of cattle over the grassland.

In Australia, the savannah is hot and dry. Few people live there.

It is a long way to a big city.

16

Some people on the savannah live in mining towns.

Others live on ranches. They raise cattle or sheep.

Long ago, Aborigines (ab-uh-RIJ-uh-neez) were the first people to live in Australia. Today, some still live on the savannah.

19

Koala

Eucalyptus (yoo-kuh-LIP-tuhs) trees grow here. Koalas (koh-AH-luhz) sleep in the branches. They eat the leaves.

Kangaroos rest in the shade. They look for small plants and grasses to eat.

Kangaroo

24

The tallest grasses in the world grow in Asia. Heavy rains flood this land each year.

Tigers and rhinos live
in this savannah. So do
leopards and elephants.

Tiger

People live here, too. They farm and raise animals.

People work to take care
of savannahs. They want
to protect the plants and
animals that live there.

Savannahs are special grasslands.

Words You Know

baobab tree

kangaroo

koala

savannah

tiger

zebras

Index

About the Author

Dr. Linda Bullock lives in Austin, Texas, on the tip of a prairie, which is another kind of grassland.

Photo Credits

Photographs © 2003: Dembinsky Photo Assoc.: 11 (Wendy Dennis), 9, 31 bottom right (Adam Jones), 3 (Stan Osolinski), 26, 31 bottom left (Anup Shah), 16 (Joe Sroka), 20, 30 bottom right (Martin Withers); Dinodia Picture Agency: 27 (N.G. Sharma), 24; Peter Arnold Inc.: 12 (Mark Edwards/Still Pictures), 29 (Still Pictures); Photo Researchers, NY: 19 (Bill Bachman), 13 (Bildarchiv/ OKAPIA), 28 (Mark Boulion), 6, 30 top (Christian Grzimek/OKAPIA), 22 (Tom McHugh), 10 (John Moss); The Image Works/Topham: 5, 31 top; TRIP Photo Library: 15 (T. Knight), cover (D. Saunders); Woodfin Camp & Associates: 23, 30 bottom left.